Cover art by Christopher Mudgett

www.ChristopherMudgett.com

CO.Y? books

Empty Cups

Early Works by Coy G. Koehler

Co.Y? Books
3940 Laurel Canyon Blvd. #708
Studio City, CA, 91604

info@whycoy.com
whycoy.com

CONTENTS

SPILT WHISKEY

Empty Cups

Early Works By Coy G. Koehler

An Introduction: Early Works, Later Memories

Within my journeys, through the ups and downs, over mountainous terrains of laughter, calamity, and lunacy, I had written these poems and had found that it was a direction wayward back to my heart. Driven sometimes by personal tragedy, philosophical observations, or revelations lost in thought, the poetry became a footprint of my history. As time wore these bones thin and the end started the beginning, I had later found that the poems were still molded by the mud that I had trekked long ago to understand this world.

I had created an atlas of my adventures with loosely quipped memoirs. Between the miles spent living, I would stop to rest my head at a diner or a dim lit bar to write without much care except to relieve myself of the day's end. With much madness in disposition of mannerisms, most of the poems had ended with the worth of a casual spill of whiskey or a coffee ring. The poems were a memory left on the page, stained by ink and vice.

So much of the poetry was tainted and forgotten by the wild excursions of life that the poetry needed to be revisited. I needed to know where I had gone. But while most of the time editing these poems, I wished that I didn't.

It was an intense wandering. Frightening at times because of the passionate angst or unrequited desire, I had to face a mountainous history of absence and change. Questions had arose; did I really surmise myself in such a way, why did I even bother to suppose my intuitions of emotion, how did I find the courage within my imagination to blindly consider such pessimistic possibilities, how far did I go anyways? Yet in drudge of all the miles with a seemingly disregarded mindfulness, there was also an encouragement and sincerity that was held steadfast and true. Moments of pure direction for love (hate) exceeded any prediction that was ever aborted. It had led my heart with encouragement to carry on through a bleak strong wind of reality.

In contemplative reflections during my editing, I understood that I needed to transcend above the disposition of my past and learn from its delusions and meaning, yet I couldn't eradicate the foregoing poems and nor did I want too. What I understood of the poems were the most poisonous and promising memories that I had created while crossing the poetic terrain. The selections were traveled and beaten.

These early poems of expeditions and later in memory were selected and separated into two chapters. Divided by the soiled pages of coffee or whiskey, the chosen poems had either displayed a gentle breeze or a hard wind, a placid afternoon or a rancid evening, a love or a lover. They were dualistic by nature's course, which I had walked.

The first chapter, Coffee Rings, is a relatively tame escapade. It should be read as an easy Sunday in the park or a cold rainy day with a mug of warm coffee. For the most part, that was how the majority of the poems from this chapter were written. Spilt Whiskey, the second chapter, embodies the opposite experience. It is a derived hell from uncontrived times, and at other times, it is a contrived misery from my thoughts that were out of context and out of mind. These poems gest a candle lit room with a bottle of Irish whiskey and ice, or they could be read possibly in a corner of a bar, hidden from the carried voices of debauch and early Saturday nightfall. But in all, these chapters were a truthful and open passage to the soul of me. They were meant to be explored but never followed, understood but never conquered, dreamt but never awakened.

With poetry molding the footprints, I've found the whole of a very lost and strange trip. So until the next journey over the emotional mountains of madness and through the valleys of a dreamer's reverie, I hope you enjoy *Empty Cups* and fill it with imagination.

Thank you very much for reading,
Coy G. Koehler

COFFEE RINGS

$1.95

Fake
flowers
and
coffee cups
hold the silence
in the morning light,
which is shining
through the stained glass
that's stained by nicotine.

My feelings
are as numb
as the hum
from the ceiling fan.

I can't read
the morning paper
because I already know the future.
Samantha told me about it yesterday,
but
now
she's dead.

The waitress
gives me the check.

And as I put out my cigarette,
I forget why I even bother to care.

Constitution

We
need protection against mankind
because neither man will ever be kind.

People
want to be led into
a promised land, but
this land, this world, needs
a promise
to know peace
without any broken pieces
and to see the real truth
that is pledged with
any allegiance
to any
flag, any
country, any
race, and any
real
reason
to
be
a
human.

Given

Sometimes
things
are always
whirling and turning
in the
summer sunshine
with reflections of smiles
given
for no reason, and at other
times, things are piercing
black monoliths of reality
that protrude justification
for rules and regulations
made fraudulent by pigs,
who feed off of stinginess
and persuasion of liaisons
in corporate contracted lie
that cut against ultimatums
given
for a change
by simplicity and beauty
as a cool
easy
breeze.

Mom

You are the one
that only
remembers
me
free
while
shitting my pants,
shitting on society,
shitting on the world
that was
never born to love anyone.

I picked purple flowers for you
when I was little because I loved you.

That day
I will always remember,
and I will always remember you,
Mom.

Snow

She wore
a grey beret
and
also
an everlasting softness
that had veiled an essence
of a passionate bliss to warm my eyes.

Naked,
I had to keep
walking home
against this long winter's wind.

Coy

It's so much easier
to paint the sky's sunshine than
to view that the sky as forgotten
my eyes.

It's so much easier
to hear a mourning dove than
to remember the harmony of
my love.

It's so much easier
to act as though I love than
to forget the hate to reason
my life.

It's so much easier
to write this poem than
to say that I'll miss you,
Coy.

Good Night, My Dear

I'll love you tomorrow
if you will never forget
how much the moon shines tonight.

Being alive
is just
the mirror of being
reflected
by what shines;
a sun,
your face,
my love.

Anyways,
I'll hide on the
shadowed side of the moon
for you to gaze with an inquisitiveness.

Good night, my dear.

More or Less

Unless you draw a triangle,
a circle will always be square.

Unless you understand yourself,
you will then always be restrained.

Unless all of the mountains crumble,
we haven't a choice but to harmonize.

Unless we speak,
we won't know anything.

Soaked

Wrenching out
cries of hopelessness,
I loosen the restrain
to become emancipated
from the predictable intensions of fools,
who forgot themselves in drowning voids
of self-deprecation and slow bereavement.

Spirit is cleansed with revelation!

My eyes are open to daydream
and dance with a visionary motion, dig.

Even though rain beats
down in its cold presence,
I appreciate its passing
and its beautiful freedom.

Man,
I'm soaked.

A Numinous Mountain

Imagining beyond the destiny
hidden by time, we believe
that what is seen by
sky
to stars
to a sunrise breeze blowing
softly across our souls
is only a vision
of love.

Soundless,
we hear.

Bold,
blinded,
beautiful,
and boundless
we
are
as a mountain
laden with clay and sage,
molded by air, water, and sealed
by flame
to
grow.

Seer believe,
we see.

Differing

Do I have to know not the differing
between the two that became one of two?
As do I have to know not the scarring
that spliced us apart with thirst for skin?
It is in simple need to live and to love.
It is in our complex yearn to want love.
I am here as you were there to believe
that we were where we were supposed to be,
but what cuts us in two are these questions
that I have to ask over and over:

Do you truly love me or only you?
Do I love you truly and only you?

Growth

Long ago,
nobody knew
what you grew up
to become,
you.

Like a wild weed
wild in the sunshine,
in an empty field,
you yielded
only love
for
life without a purpose
except to add and be nothing but free.

In dying days to come,
you still will become
you, the child that
was born to die
in the sunshine
alive and kind
without an
underlay
of lies
that
just
are.

Dew drops under the moonlit night,
I will sleep until they are dry today.

Nautical

A mermaid glistening in a pearl blue hue
with her faintly painted and breezed bare skin
laced and enwrapped by lost floating leaves of the sea.
She coyly
flounders about in folly
afloat on the ocean's foamed veil,
in
so
to
tempt the yearn of a sailor's manhood
or the love of a pirate's past lust.

A lonesome seafarer's eye longing for shore
to land his ridden bones, to light his archaic pipe,
and to lay his thoughts like stoical cliffs crashed by tide.
He wanes
weathered without
any maiden adrift
upon the ocean's vast trail,
in
so
to
threat
the heal of a life experienced
or the fear of a quest forgotten.

A sun settling slowly to uncover the moon's guidance
and to adorn the mystery of navigated constellations
for a fabled star-crossed love to be written in sand.
Seducing in raptured innocence with beckoned whisper,
which caresses airily across the crest of waves, she

echoes inside the dispirited and broke mariner's ear,
"Relax, my boatman. You will rest now; here with me
amongst a gentle kelp of my covering, in so to dream
with the wind forever a sail and never without fail."
His old salt became distraught by coddling bitter in
ale of delusion, so he unbounded his anchor that had
tied his cradle ashore and sailed toward her gracing
cadence under dimmed lit fallen stars to bathe and
believe in her aquatic benevolence that she promised.
Awaiting patiently, she sings a song of melodic hymn
so he can dance a foul and follow the darken billows
that lay way and swell in delight for their pleasure.
Alas, he sees his heart in reflection of the sea and
commands with a fierce yet atoned resonance for love,
"I am here now, my beautiful creature. I am willing
to dare your eyes and rest only on bosom, in so to
dream indefinite by sail without fail amidst our sea."

And then kisses like a mutiny aboard a ship,
they were cast away eternally by Neptune's spear
into a crevasse of love's lost oblivion,
into the bliss of an abyss to drown.

Statue

These words
remain neglectful from
my truth:

Love
Promise
Life

Those words
endure uncertainty by
endless judgments shaped
as
clay
sculpted
for magnificence
to collapse and corrode
by time's delicate hand.

Left rotted in your garden,
my stoical truth will remain.

A Boy

Flying far from above the way that I was, I wasn't
alone,
but that
was seen
somewhere
between my dreams and all of these nightmares.

Directions

Which direction did you want to go?

Remember deviations are only growth.
Remember dreams are only nostalgia left astray.
Remember illumination is only seen in shadows.
Remember explanations only become judgments.
Remember decisions are only created.

Whatever direction you go, you go.

Her

Her
voice echoes throughout my ethereal imaginings
aloof with amusement under this sullen moonlight.

Her
shyness exalts indecent contempt of judgment
to kiss long the subtle bareness below an ear.

Her
graces fool fools, those for shallow thoughts;
into failure, any man falls bewildered by try.

Her
essence divulges a secret deep in evening air
as a shadow that is guided by beauty to lips.

Her
subtle displacing of simple soft let limbs and
airy like hair becomes fair for me to traverse.

Her
tempered reactions tussle to spite against par
as tristful eyes overlook her proposal in style.

Her
eyes lay on me to wonder of her seduction within
a gentle wrath that is fiercely worth a deity's lust.

Her
innocent flower blooms easy into the darkest sky;
And in an open bed, she is the only flower that I will love.

Never and Ever

Love
is never
pretty unless
someone loves
you, otherwise it's
just a bunch of fables
written by lost wanders
looking for what was never
love.

Love
isn't ever
useless; petty
until somebody
you otherwise deny
within words of a story
written inside a lost analogy
which reads what you will ever
love.

Stillbirth

A birth, now death, still
inside the mother's lone womb.
Inside the father,
a love and a valiant
still reasoning of their life.

Winter

When
the wind
blows its cold white bone coil
around the skin sought for vocation,
then the spine
stops
in fear
to understand reason
and decision
for direction
until the next season
to envelop faith and growth
to live again and
to die again by another ill emotionless wind.

Death decides,
life abides, and
love hides itself within the sheltered warmth of dreams.

A Glimpse

something to believe in
is sunshine glistening in

the corner of your eye

that you are peeking out
of to see me leaving out

the reason for my eye

Dog

Living
with
war weighs
heavy with consequences.

Like
pitted dogs,
we were born
into this caged world
to hate each other indefinitely,
but
why
would you
choose to kill or to be killed ?

Never let
anything discourage
you from your courage
to love and not to fight.

We are all free to hide
inside of the daisy flowers
and chase all of the butterflies
because, like the dogs that we are,
everyone loves to get their tummy rubbed
sometime.

Bark, don't bite.

Hum

Dawn breaks a quick soft sky across the street
from where I sit; I drink, and then I drift.
A humming bird flies by so high, so sweet,
from where I wit; it dips, and then it shifts.
My heart in beat does not know why I fair
for thirst, for eyes, for curse; in shame, I bow.
This err and innocence will always dare
the lot of what should not be but by why.
Someday, will we part and then mend in death
so to know it all yet know all that stings?
Or come together to share our own breath
with birth, to share the truth of everything?

Now I sleep but only to dream of you
in hopes that you awake to deem me true.

Observance

Observance
in red,
my eyes
tend to seed
a breath of yearn
for something that
I can't escape from.

I turn and heed to
an artificial recollection
of contempt for beauty
because there isn't room
in this dim lit place
to care
for what I know to be authentic.

I see blinded by tomorrow.

Summer Solstice

Inhaling
the mystic
red earth's
sun-beaten scent
from lush sage bushes
blossoming as a season's
wisdom and folly begins its solstice,
I walk.

Following in time,
I
fall in love
with everything that is.

A Love Letter

Tears
stained the paper
that I had written
worthless words upon.

They found an eternity
in
the ink
that had bled
to a period for an end.

A love letter now lost, forever.

Dreaming?

Die
to try and never
try to die
because you're going to die
anyways.

Live
to die and never
die to live
because you're going to die
anyways.

Any which way
is anyway to which you are, so
pinch yourself because
the
dream
is
real.

Ink

It
was
written
in the wind.
Words flew off the paper and seeded imagination.

Why
should
I write my thoughts?

Why
should
anyone care about my love?

Why
should
I dream anymore?

Untamed and liberated, I grew. A mind
matured high and natural,
and then I understood
that
these
roots
of soul
could seed s ome one else 's im .a.. gin At I? o.. n.

Path

When spirit is lost
and revered, then time
begins its perish and lonely trials of history.

Imagined
by imagination,
you are expected to be
and accepted to leave
by the grace of your own
fall because one mountain
has many directions descending.

This liberty
is without any hope, but
it is also without any consequence
to suffer any reason that we have to live.

Thousands

A thousand spirits
followed
the sage plains,
and a
thousand died by the
possessed black snake
that slithered
as old
mud
to
conquer and erase history.

It was determined
by a false direction
that the hunt
for
those that
thought immortality was moral
throughout
our fertile mother was but a savaged disease.

These thousand spirits still live.
These thousand spirits, still, haunt
the
great
eternal
native plains.

A Sunday Stroll

Leaves
from the trees
puff by my bare feet
in the California fall air.

My boots
had been broken
by my being broke,
but maybe
a dime can get me
a cup of coffee
or the three of cups
from the psychic down the street?

I guess,
I can remember
your phone number
tomorrow
to call
because
today is Sunday
or at least
I think
it
is?

Earplugs

As I'm eavesdropping
and engulfing
excruciating
loathing
towards
you,
I sit
still
listening
to you and pray that
you choose the color yellow
for your new Hummer, that your
boyfriend stops sleeping around,
your mother gets the house, that you
finally get that plastic surgery you wanted,
and that you make it to your hair appointment
with that gorgeous "gay" guy that you want to
make
straight because he has the tightest and cutest
little ass
that you've ever seen,
all before you die,
real soon.

Joshua

I gave you my tears,
so you took them as a thief,
smiled forever.
But as words, we are only
here to assume our life.

Photograph

white
and
black
as
white
was black

my love is forever held within a moment of
amazement

black
and
white
as
black
was white

breathless is her silhouette wispily sliding to the
window

Underwear

Sometimes,
my heart
is here or there,
never over there
nor over here;
here, where
it
should be.

It
should be
beating strong,
singing a song, or
screaming aloud
with absolute
amazement
and excitement
for the world,
to the world,
and into the world,
instead of being
isolated from the world
inside
my lonely corner
of
my own world that I
created
in a universe of
never ending love,
thoughts of
words to say forever,

and
imaginary ideas of
what this
world
is
according to me
because
I do only agree with me
and what the me, me, and me
has to say about
my
heart
that is hiding
under
there.

Under where?

Ha,
I said
underwear.

Abyss

Envisioning
the abyss
in between realities
of resolution
is this convoluted process
that has become
an inevitable fate for destiny,
but
what remains
isn't
what is momentous
for
the journey.

So, carry headlong into the open wild.

Endless Conflict

Slaughter the child, let the mother see.
Slaughter this wild, let our mother see.

To the black day,
another body dead
and lost in innocence
by the luring lies of trust.

To the red sun,
another sacrifice
left in pain with blood
for the soulless feast
that has yet to be tasted.

To the gray shadow,
another shaded area
in accomplished greed
and the falsified need
for flesh and adulterated
land that was surrendered.

To the white face,
another hope and
challenge to overcome
the young and the old
by revealing the myths
that have been spoken
for over thousands of years.

Slaughter the child, let the mother see.
Slaughter this wild, let our mother see.

Listen

Tongues echo
through my mind
as
I think
with anguish
for
reasons
why I am
and why you
are the only sound
that I want to hear,
but
as my breath trembles,
my fear
tells me the truth
that you will never be near.

So,
I scream
without a sound,
without a voice never to be found.

Precipitation

Beginning
the day
with
gray
skies
falling
into rain,
the reign
of loneliness
tends to conquer
my will to accept a bitter defeat.

Patter-patter
Patter-patter
Patter-patter

The tragic clouds
covet and console
my contemptuous state of mind.

Patter-patter
Patter-patter

Thunder follows the prophetic lighting.

Patter-patter
Patter-patter
Patter-patter

And as rain drops
from
my
drained
and tired woes,
my tears
immerse
into puddles
that reflect the past
from present problems.

Patter-patter
Patter-patter

Vanished

Her
silent beauty
in ethereal slumber
gently glides from vision
across the cherry blossom petals.

A whispered movement
summoned a slight turn of head to marvel
and follow without any judgment presented
except a notion that had dwindled as the zephyr.

Then she disappeared.

An apparition
downed itself in subtle guidance
and possessed my flesh to chase
an indecision
with fearful excitement exuding
an impossibility.

Then I disappeared.

Brooding woes weary
this rapture of belief in love
without ever a trial.
Guilty before associated
with any innocence of demeanor,
I swallow my raw pride relentlessly
and smile.

Then we had disappeared.

Again

Again,
a day
was
spent
and drained
by everyday
with every thought of you,
but
I don't even know who you are.

Maybe you are just
another feeling of something
that could have been true,
yet my dreams are really better
than anyone's reality.

So
go
away
because I know again
everyday
is
today.

Dreary wisdom
filled today by believing
that these bones
were only made to be broken
with my heart
that was only meant to be felt
and never given,

again.

Ephemeral

I
thought to softly kiss
her white velvet neck
from behind her eyes.

From behind her eyes,
I saw essence poised as
a woman in a natural and boundless
fluttering bewilderment of innocence.

I
thought to seize her lips
to never let that moment go.

From behind her eyes,
I could see the possibilities
of her
and
I
alone
amongst
a moon yet to rise.

I
thought to whisper her ear
with small words of childish love.

From behind her eyes,
I saw myself
in the wrong
to daydream
of soulful trials with desire
and to escape from heaven with her wonderment.

I
thought, but that was all.

Longhand

Write a
drama!

Write a
novella!

Write a
Tanka!

Write!
Write!
Write words, words, words!

Or, just write a suicide note.

Rain Gutter

Fluidity
falls
in
and
then
drips
down to the ground
with a sound that is
similar
to that
of
echoes.

Rusted
by agony
and pollution,
repeated by a
seasonal killing
in cycles of deception,
the rain
will never
stop
for
us;
we need
to
stop for the rain.

Water Rat

I wish
I could've
breathed in
the beginning running water droplet
that had first engulfed the drenched earth
to taste it,
to drown in its oceans, streams, and reign.

I would be forever free
by means of being forever.

I would know what no one knows
by not knowing what no one knows.

I would be me by just being me, water.

"Empty your mind;
be formless,
shapeless, like water.

If you put water into a cup, it becomes the cup;
you put water into a bottle, and it becomes the bottle;
you put it in a teapot, it becomes the teapot.

Now, water can flow or it can crash. Be water my friend."
-Bruce Lee

American Breakfast

An
ignorant
egghead
cracked
into
an omelet
of his own.

Hamming
it up like the pig
he is,
he
slices and dices,
thinking
he's hot cakes,
but
he's just a side of burnt toast.

Check, please!

Eternal

Wilted flowers kept in a book
without a face.

Faded colors
faded into pages.

Wasted by tears
of pleasure, the agony
and anger became the illusion.

Another night
near the end
and
near the edge
of a still pond,
she awaits silent
within a moment
to drown all
sorrows
in the reflection
of another
radiant sphere
soon to be
opaque by a
second thought
to late.

Goodbye, angel.

Lost

Fall leaves
waltz in the sunshine
as I gaze in awe
of this bewilderment
in realization
that I may have a future
with you.

Decisions
should never be made
with sounds
still trickling
its music from the creek,
so I walked away to listen
for the silence.

Moss on wood
and all of these things
that I could have done
fall apart
as time has it to be.

Thoughts
gruel over
how many times
I had walked in this circle.

Maybe it is time
because I have never found a way out.

Glare

Glaring
into the past of what
I was supposed to believe
to be true,
I even now think
of
unforgiving
attributes that refute allocations
against anyone who was deemed honorable
because our history is dissonant and distant from fact.

The fact
that false identity replaces
an infant's eye with soldiers' blood,
a nurses' tear, and some gods' excuse
to kill
disgusts me like the maggots breathing inside a corpse.

We stab the backs of men,
so we can survive the world
which is as lonely as a reading chair
and as empty as the book that people pretend to believe
in.

Destiny is marked by erosion and judgment,
which has been burdened by millions of cries
from eyes glaring into periods of hell that we
had constructed by
flesh, gluttony, and ignorance.

We hold a weapon to vision
rather than a vision as a weapon for truth.

I stare without hope for everyone,
who is blinded by the dealings of
our everyday sewage with useless
meetings and casual propaganda
mumbled in constipation of spin.

I cross my heart in hopes to die
because there is a needle in my eye
from all of the
indecent, incredible,
and ill input of credence
from our commander of chief,
who quacks like the lame ugly duckling.

Our eyes are open now,
but our mouths are still shut
from the threats of intimidation
undermining conscious with sporty intuition of fear.

We, the people,
need a leader
who knows to lead
with prosperity,
civility, and, above all, reality.

I, the blind, can see.

Wedded

Nevermore is now
forever more in between
their dreams and their love.

An Afternoon

Speaking with voices
that I cannot hear anymore
at a table inside the coffee shop,
I saw your eyes painted by the daylight.

Illuminating likeness to a kiss
was a reason for me
to know why
I still hide in
shadows
of
windows
opened for the breeze to flow
free.

"Hi, my name is Coy"

Figurine

The effigy of love was chiseled in my mind.

Breaking the
stone with thought,
I
sculpted an ignorant creation of another.

From pieces
of disappointment,
I
created an absent masterpiece of another.

With glazed eyes
filled with possibilities,
I
tarnished the statue for virtue of another.

Then after the elimination, its beautification,
and my personification, my mind completed
love's
indecent and grotesque display of someone else's
effigy.

Many Mountains

How
many
steps
to the
top of this mountain?

Seclusion,
I see within me
my will to become
as vast as the vision
that stands before my feet,
that stand with my hands
soaring high towards the sun
in question.

But when
all this is
said and done,
what
will be,
will be
just me
seeing the path
that I had climbed up to the top.

Many miles,
many steps,
and many thoughts
have led me to see many mountains.

Seer

I won't see you
tomorrow,
too sorrow.

I won't see you,
so believe,
so be a leaf.

Anyways,
any days,
I will see you.

Farwell,
be well,
I will see you.

I see you.

Where?

Where can I find you?

As you hide from yourself,
I question myself.
Seeking for you inside a dream,
I hope that I can awake.
Understanding the moon as a reflection,
I wonder if you're the sun.
As the trees whirl into a whispering current,
I cannot see the air yet I do feel;
are you the gentle breath which carries me into the
spinning heavens?

Where can I find you?

As Us

                As
   borders,   flags, and
   countries   inhibit our
   freedoms,   lives,
   justices,   and
capabilities   with antagonistic
   reasons,   we're limited by
regulations,   political
  prejudices,   bias
   religions,   and gluttonous
enterprises,   which determines our
 conscious,   our
   choices,   and our
  destinies;   the end of
                us.

Ghost

Desperate winds
cry
from the hollows
of another
life.

Spirit
understands the stand
of self dividing one's thought
into
two
like a tree
branching out to the sky, moon, and sun.

Yet, still is the wind in answer of my question and love.

Missing

Straight
and bliss

To wonder under sun

Directions
ruin
any venture

My pockets held the rain for a day

Subtle realities

Humble in undertones of living

Lavender eyes

Rivers of people

I began to play music with the dissipating clouds

Harmonious miles
across
the harrowed land

Starlings swarm from the distance between sight
and sound

Let it go

Lead it gone

She Loves Me But Not

Spoken
and broken,
my words slide off of
my
tainted
tongue
onto the paper
that is tarnished
by my tears trickling
down from
deciding
my life,
my
life.
I
sigh
just to think
of another reason
to be alive,
so I have
to lie
to you
because I have
no reason
to be
like
the reflection
that you want to see in
your
own
mirror.

Window

I loved you
when you looked
into yesterday's window
and saw it
as it was,
yesterday.

Our times have changed.

Our hearts have changed.

I loved you
when you locked
it,
our window.

SPILT WHISKEY

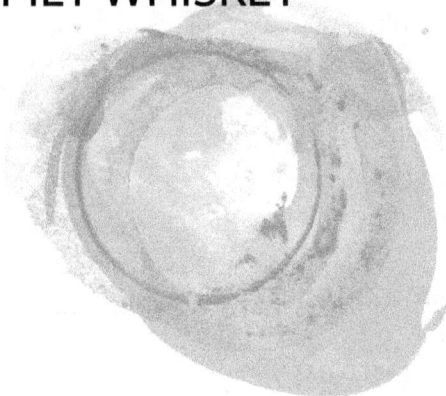

Blue in the Face

Nothing
is as significant
than
what isn't,
so
never wonder
what it is
when it is
always magnificent.

Scream loud until blue
so to
let your face bare true.

I, Now.

Disgusted
by the winds that change,
the sea that is so estranged,
and the enormous sting sensed
from the days
I had thought
that being
thoughtful
was worth what it was worth,
I, now,
see how I am.

Worms always dry in the sun.

Words, in all ways, die for love.

Digested
by the wrongs of shame,
the pleas from the deranged,
and the righteous fictitiousness
of people when
they were someone
at some point without having any point,
I, now,
see who I am.

Only a Flock of Feathers

I'm tired of listening to
your circles of thought
and what you naught
and sought
to do
because the birds do fly but only because they are up
high.

Look down at
your own feet
because
two plus two
is way too many
for someone who said that they are only just being
human.

So please,
again,
don't tell me
of your woes
and worries
because I'm only flying in the immense blue vulnerable
sky.

Snakes

Friends
have become
fiends
that had fallen from trust
into the pit
of love
of self
to deceive as snakes
coiling in fear from their dark
and hopeless eyes.

Lies quickly strike the throat
and draw blood without ever knowing the truth.

Deadly the venom of assumption and greed can
seethe and spread into the heart of an innocent.

How many times
did you tell me that you loved me?

Bask in the sun,
find shade when the day is done,
and know that you will never love anyone.

And as you slither back into the wallowing hole
that you had created for shelter from the world,
remember
that
you're alone
to devour your own tail.

Your (You're Love) Love

No one will listen
to your
pain
because
it's never heard
from within your soul;
it's as a foreign echo or
a forgotten dream in the morning.

Your happiness
is as empty;
it's
only filled by
temporary gold
and shallow memories.

The fear
that shatters
yourself, your art,
the mirror that no one will see,
is as the wind
from a falling feather
that hasn't any direction except to
land
and lie.

Your hate
is in solitary confinement,
locked behind your imagination,
and sentenced without
a life to believe.

All of your emotions
are as worthless as your birth.

All of your dreams
are as worthless as your death.

All of your love is real.

18 Wheels

Wheedle.
Wheel.
Needle.
Need.

He continued to drive
unmoving
at a truck stop
in the back
of
his
rig while
rigging it up
to shut up it all.

In.
Out.
Fried.
Eggs.

His next drop
was in 10 more miles,
but his head had dropped off
long before he could even make it.

Dawn.
Sunshine.
Prostitute.
Constitution.

She slashed
his tires after
he refused to pay
for the unleaded gas.

Road.
Know.
Go.
Empty.

Now, another mile is left
before he can leave
everything
at the loading dock
inside his loaded mind.

Wife.
Wild.
Knife.
Child.

Home at last.
He grabs a beer,
watches the boob tube,
and then passes out until
his next run
to
nowhere.

Catch Wild

Cold
nights
kindled our
thoughts, senseless.

Near
our sought love,
spinning and pining for life,
we
started the fire
that we had first began
before yesterday
to
catch wild.

Pissing
in the snow,
pissing off
the neighbors,
and then pissing off each other,
we pissed on the world.

In Tempo

Doesn't that slap
beat
say play that smack?

Doesn't that tang
taste
like a fresh onion bang?

These questions cannot be retorted until
the last shadow drifts into the twilight lights,
and those answers cannot be questioned until
the next morning bird song plays
with an unknowing yet tempting
liberty to believe
without
a
mind
or care.

Slow and low,
You should always speak of what you already
know.

…Or Else

Sweetness is somewhere
else.

I long for something
else.

Someone
else
is for whoever
else.

So elsewhere,
I will find you amid
the white crisp soft served sheets
of a creamed and whipped dream
waiting in melted memory for me.

Coda

For
eleven nights,
I screamed for your love.

Now
for four
more months,
you will not be able to love me.

Then at that minute, we'll see
the three muses
interchange
into
our
one
Moon
for us to be composed as a symphony of passion.

Just

I looked up to the cosmos
on the road
for that certain release,
but tonight I was trying
to see something
that couldn't
just
subsist
in means of means.

Damn this madness of living,
although this madness is living.

Oh well,
such as hell,
my heaven, me, is
just
human.

100%

1%,
what
is this
mockery
that's always
a monarchy disguised as
a harlequin of democracy?

A jester of court in corporations
sought to entertain with binary
corruption, politics, and envious greed.

To ride high upon elephants and mules
in the parade of gluttonous hierarchy
while reciting integrated monologues
of disinformation on a political stage of satires,
which have only been erected in these recent eras
for egotistical potbellied empires to hide behind
governed curtains, so we, the people, will blindly applaud
the opening act to our tragedy with deaf ears and hail the
one percent that appoints delegation with gross
parodies.

Your nobles are too frighten to twaddle
about accountability, adages, and abuse.

Your servants are rising against
the fraud, finances, and fiction.

Kings and queens are falling
from truth, trial, and taxes.

99%
of
this "kingdom"
is crumbling
from gold
turned
into
paper,
words
that
turned
into
fables,
and our
sacrifices
that turned
into self-righteous upscale excesses with pointless
indignations
toward a nation's honest sovereignty for a harlequin
whore who
does not deserve the represented dignity except for its
ignorant
folly of jest in fat ballooned gods that we should
sightlessly trust.

Passion's Crime

Love
sacrifices
faith
by
trust
for
one another to understand
one another
insofar
as
to
unite
under a
universal law, unlawfully.

And as thieves wild in the night,
we escape from this life's decree.

Starlight

Empty bottles
hollowed by empty thoughts,
the thirsty tongues lick
the nectar of lost nights and new sorrows.

Twilight mixes shade
as the mix settles from stir.

I sit with reflective conquering
in front of spirits deemed hopeless
for tomorrow's dream inside of a
demon's juggling act that beckons
for
a smile
for
awhile
until
the curtain comes down
and the house lights come up.

The crickets play their song "Goodnight, Starlight".

A Black Hole

I'm spinning
in my own
galaxy.

Dancing
to melodies
set to explode
as
the sun flares fly
in a space- hot spin,
I groove
in atmospheric spheres
as the stars in rainbows
collide
with the moons
of the empty, cold, and alone.

My mind, my own,
is deep in a black hole
and
free from form
in an asteroid aesthetic, so
you better
look
out
man!

I'm soaring wild
in the solar wind
without the twilight

or a sunset to know
when
the day
or
the night
will ever begin
for the party
to never
end.

Cut

Like a blade, I had
forgot who I cared for; you?
My true love? You are.

Know One

Was it worth
the fabrication?

Polished by soulless words
and wishing that your face
was
hidden
from everyone,
you should have
known that you're no one.

But, you didn't know
that your corruption
was also an honest
perception
with
karma
only being a circle
in your imagination
that spirals indefinite
for everyone
else
that knows "one", no one.

Perfection

Somewhere in between the emptiness
and some sort of contempt in reality,
I decided to walk down an alleyway,
which was
deranged and arranged
within an
alternate
placement of pure perfection
called
chaos.

Everything is perfect because everything is not.

Sunk

Void of thought,
I began to rot away
like the drifting wood in wallow.

Forgiveness is a joke
when blindness is the only hope.

Now, these visions
are washed away by the waves
because of what it seemed to be
was just another rumored lie for me to know
what's
deep below.

Sometimes it hurts
like currents crashing
against my throat.

My will to survive
became a thrill
to hide
from all of those lies
because these dreams
will be washed away by the waves
anyways.

Just another whispered truth for me to know
what's
deep below
inside of me.

A Celebrity's Brevity

Bleak eyes
shone bright
without regard for anyone.

You walked
through the door
without knowing where you were.

You had talked
as you were important enough,
but just like every other person,
the real star shines
within the corner of everyone else's eye
that no one ever sees without a compassionate view.

So
sorry,
I could care, but
I couldn't care less.

So
no,
I don't know
who you "are".

So
go
away, thank you.

Domestic

Slap- Mom

"Why do you even care?"

Slap- Dad

"This over, god damn it!"

Slap- Reality

Another
slammed door
echoing far into tomorrow,
a thrown trinket shattered
and left for dead,
and once more,
fallen tears are replaced
on the shelf of broken memoirs
and domestically abused hope.

"Daddy?"

Laurel Canyon Boulevard

Sometimes,
I
look
forward
back
down
the street
as day to a night,
but as too many nights
to a day,
I look
forward
to just getting back home.

Plain View

To escape
free from her ecstasy,
explains her
pleasure in pain,
a hopeless void
decided
in an
illusion
of desired torment.

Everybody knows
since she thinks that nobody
can know
her.

Shun by shouldn't,
she should of seen it.

A shallow sorry
and another shady Friday,
she walks wasted and lost again.

Someday, she will see the lit azure skies as free as she can
see herself
alone and under a deep sleep of her own darkness and
bliss to dream
against the wave's crash, against the world, and against
the life that she will never know reasons for, even though
it is there in plain view.

Thorns

S
h
e
had
l
a
i
d
her
r
o
s
e
down
g
e
n
t
l
y
for me to
s
e
e.
Exiled
by amazement
and allurement,
blooming of purity
and absolute mystery,
her rose became my
rapture.

A Conversation with Myself

For what? It's my hell.

Iridescent tears swelled like the soft waves set to crash
and tremble with a fierce thrashing immensity against
my weakened jowl that is forced to howl for no reason
than another full idiotic moon emulating the sun's fire.

For what? It's my hell.

What the hell do you think? Your revolving
evolvement into a new moon disguises a truth.
Where does your brilliance come from? A lie?

For what? It's my hell.

My spirit had always found me laughing inside the
destitute bowels of starvation; bloated and worth
for the vultures, I always condemn myself for mute
reasons which are as aloof as the tears that fall.

For what? It's my hell.

What the hell should you think? Again, all of this
life is empty, so by humble famine, you will perish for
others to feast judgmentally on your heart because they
themselves are only willed by vanity and arrogant fat.

For what? It's my hell.

I lost my will more than twenty years ago, so once more,
yesterday was not another day anew; I will bar my eyes,

my mouth, and anything else that I had left wide open for people to use in ruling me an instrument for their will.

It's my hell.

Don't Touch

flesh was found outside
it will always be inside

memories

shielding her sister
she cried for her mother
shoving away her brother
she killed her father

glass became a knife

now

the holidays belong
to a widowed wife

memories

don't touch
daddy plays nice
don't touch
it's our secret
don't touch
don't tell your mother

tears will never tell the truth

innocence died with a touch

memories

Leave

Looking
for the past,
looking backwards
through broken glass,
we believed
the light burning for our desire.

Seeking is not everything
when being naked and wild
is our freedom to sing aloud
that our life is not our fault!

We dreamt.
We made love.

Creating within a vision
and forgetting motive by
a certain tempted wisdom,
I will always
witness
judgment
inside of our breath
as a kiss.

Now, it's time for you to leave.

Read Between the Thighs

HERE,
don't believe,
AN AMAZING OFFER
in television.
NEW AND IMPROVED
like a slab of flesh,
100% GRADE "A" MEAT
filled with lies and gluttony
WITHOUT SHIPPING AND HANDLING
and a coffin.

IF YOU ACT NOW,
which is what they want you to do,
YOU CAN GET ANOTHER ONE FOR FREE
in order to be a total patsy.

ONLY FOR A LIMITED TIME
because your soul is worthless as a slave.

CALL NOW AND TALK TO OUR BEAUTIFUL SALES GIRLS
with fake breasts, no personality, and who couldn't make
it as a porn star.

1-800-YOU-SUCK

To Night

A sun
sets slow
today.

Without
my feet to carry me,
I sit near the roadside
hoping for a dream to show
me the way home,
but only
formations of lions and ships
appear above the horizon's line.

I remain now
to regain later
another
two miles with my
two feet stuck in molasses on this
two lane freeway falling to night.

Adoption

Mother's milk turned sour
with 200 roses by the hour,
but don't worry,
I'm sure
a sugar daddy
can help the bitter turn sweet
as soon as the money starts to meet
a superficial need for jewels, dresses,
and other substances to get you by and high.

Instead of trusting your self's own blood,
that was your child, you had forgotten
the worth that commends an angel's smile
and its baby's hand to hold tight.

So now,
black and blue
from
the trick
that did the damage,
the shit
that hit you under the bridge,
and the bite
of reality and its garbage,
you know love, always, was for always.

Don't worry; your daughter will be fine.

Don't

On top
of the city lights,
I stare
into the core of characters
heartless and bleak from countless
attempts of a midnight Russian roulette.

Laughter bellows
into an echo
from
behind me
in my desolation
as the wine flows
on to the street with the piss
enveloping its smell in the stairwell.

A ghost moans for understanding.

My head
hangs in low stealth motion,
a demon
without a care for anyone but you.

Please,
don't call me.

I love you.

Loins

Benevolence
is in consciousness
and in drift,
I
fall.

The night light eddies into the trees.

The cold grass bed saturates my loins.

I forgot,
but
I forgot.

Room 8

A vacant hotel room
with no vacancy.

I sit
static wondering where
I am.

It doesn't matter as it does.

Channels of television
start to channel
my thoughts,
my aggression,
my sadness, and my reality,
which is supposed to be real.

Circles on the ceiling
symbolize the obvious
of these
contemplations,
but so does the door knob.

I am out.

Viva La Revolution!

Too
many
nights
alone and cold
spent outside under
shades of starlight,
I'm starting
a new revolution
for myself to believe.

Damn this chill
creeping along my legs
to soul.

Against
all odds,
I will arise
to fight myself,
to conquer myself,
and to liberate my will!

Need to overcome this hell.
Need to oppress the oppressor.
Need to overthrow this dictator of my
self-inflicted pain and worthless struggle.

AH! HA!
Viva la revolution!
HA! AH!
I surrendered to myself!

I am my own prisoner now,
but only I know where the key is kept.

Aladdin's Madness

Beginning to leave, the end is to start.
Love, this affair is dissension afar.

One time
was worth
three wishes.

One time
was worth
three wishes.

One time
was worth
three wishes.

Our forgiveness was what we understood.
We were free hearts that were just wished away.

Downward

Sending
myself to oblivion
without integrating
any thought,
I had started
to become
aware
of you
sending
me smiles
under the table.

"Stop!"
I said, but
I forgot to open
my mouth.

So,
I put my cigarette
out
and then you took
the exit, stage right, with him.

In another evening, I'm not going to care,
but with such a futile night, I had decided
which
way
to
go.

Misplaced

Where are your words?

I saw them the other day
by
my
pillow,
but now,
they're nowhere
to be
found.

Maybe they're inside of your eyes?

Can I take a look?

Rot

The
crying eyes of children
like
fresh clear spring pools
show faith for a future
and a hope in creation ,
but
too
soon,
they become
infested with
polluted promises
that toy, rape, and bleed
with virgin dreams that beg and thrash
against wills for more thrills, more pills,
and
less
of a reason
to live
while
trying to die.

I cried. I tried.

Vomit

Ingesting the disappointment
of mobility, information, and love.

Today isn't worth the regression
of our apparent tyranny. I write.

Stop. Look. Realize. Fight. Free.

Becoming the fundamental nature that is
becoming the function of our existence is merely being
alive.

Where are the riots?
Where is your soul?

Our stomachs
are filled with the
bile of unawareness
and deception,
which we swallow
for a "better tomorrow",
but now we are sick from its greed
and slaughter for god and for gold.

Maybe I don't shut up, but I do grow up; however,
when I look at this world in its state of states,
impoverished countries, and imprudent borders, I do
throw up.

Almost Passed Out

Long days
filled with disappointment,
filled with drops
of
fine
wine.

Maybe in these days coming
I will see the sun,
the life,
and the eyes
to which you see with,
but
maybe
I will just die
so to guide you across the river's destined flow?

But
until then,
I'll remain on the floor,
next to my bed,
almost
passed
out.

Games

City
street
lights
set alight;
inside of my eyes,
a dim awareness of a killer.

Will the damn hot night ill my morning
or will it appear as desire in my bedroom?

I cannot make any more promises
except
for a
future that isn't
because another miracle
will position me fair as a pawn to the sickle.

Amusement for a muse,
I am within God's play.

My Love

A minute
in morning,
my
eyes laid you down
while wondering of
my
reach to feel anew touch.
But your limbs weren't
my
desire to trail and capture
in your morning stretch to
my
flustered decrees of rationale
and obsolete exacerbation of
my
ecstatic quest to conquer manhood,
it was the undertaking to distance
my
being with freewill and wield against all
expectations and contend to you with just
my love.

Sea Sick

Wondering in a sea
of voices
while
sailing the high tide,
I
decided
to
drown.

Drown out the world.
Drown out the laughter.
Drown out the music.
Drown out my thoughts.

Swallowing my conscious
to escape this reality of being
lost at sea,
I said...

Good night.

Vote: Yes/No

I never liked you America.
I hated your being and all of your beings;
spoiled little bitches breathing my air
with your plastic realities, you are a
desperate whore begging for more toys,
more weapons, more silicone, and more
 of what you already have but don't want anymore.

You're a rich arrogant asshole;
you're the shithead on the playground;
you're a wife who cheats on her fat husband;
you're a husband who throws dollars at a stripper,
corporate institutions, and self-righteous statues that
claim:

We, the people,
of the wealthy elite stand together as
we, the people,
watch everyone else in the country fall.

 Yes, America, I hate you.

I always liked you America.
I loved your land and the sea to shining sea;
sentient lovers dreaming among breath-taking
views of vast landscapes with freedom, you are
our loving mother begging for us to grow more,
teach more, endure more, and become more of what
you already had shown us with so much more.

You're a diverse intelligent saint;
you're an elderly couple in the park;
you're a homeless man feasting a free meal;
you're a home owner providing for a family
in small communities with self-righteous pride that
deems:

We, the people,
of this liberal state of union, know that
we, the people,
have a true understanding of compassionate truth.

Yes, America, I love you.

Waiting for 7-11 to Open

Being wild
while being not,
I remain within this
caged reality that you've
created
for
me;
I,
your
humble
servant of shit
and swallow, will obey
your T.V. reality, I will obey
your bullshit hostility, I will obey
your pretend head of sanctity, I will obey
your anything that isn't anything but mortality; I will
obey.

Dare I say that I love?

Dare I say that I am?

Dare I say anything that isn't anything but of our
mortality?

Oh, thank heaven for 7-11.

Yolanda

The wrong room, dim by blue disco lighting,
holds smoked sullen tones of paranoia;
echoes of slow sexual frustration
float above blue shag, stained by ash and blood;
the white marble table mirrors white lines
near a Golden Desert Eagle .50;
silver paisley walls are guilty of crimes,
and no one will ever get out alive;
with her opulent wet lips, she screams fire,
unconsciously naked behind dark shades;
inside an afro womb of velvet dreams,
blood drips from her sea blue-green eyelashes.

"Drink your big black cow and get out of here…"
plays in the background as she shuts the door.

Being Third Person to an Idiot

"Smile!"

Nothing troubles me
because of my bubble.

As is, is as
big as my ignorant head
that wishes everyone well.

Oh hello,
I forgot I am happy.
Oh go to hell,
I forgot I was happy
being phony.

Oh hello again, I am happy.

Have a nice day.
Have a nice day.
Have a nice day.
Have a nice day.
Have a nice day.
Have a nice day.
Have a nice day.
Have a nice day.
Have a nice day.
Have a nice day.

I Call Bullshit

I'll buy your inventions
to subside with this nauseating life
that's been created for me;
a car,
a TV,
a computer,
a toilet to shit in.

I'll shower
in your chemicals
made to purify the water,
play Marco Polo in a pool
while swallowing more chemicals,
and then surf the ocean's high tide
that is contaminated with even more chemicals.

I will demolish my will to succeed as a human
and become the consumer
that you've programmed me for
with the proceeding accommodations
brought to me by the
DEA,
FDA,
and the CIA with gratitude.

And I'll smile without contempt
while being justified
by buying into your bullshit,
your products, and your unjustified dreadful lies
so that you, provocateur of any so-called truth,

may continue to tax my existence and delegate its
turmoil

I will eliminate
my life faster for others with causation
and hope for destroying our world, species,
in so that
maybe
there will be a chance
for another organism to survive
and flourish
with peace, equality, coexistence, and, above all,
benevolence.

Because after all that has been said, read, and tried for
dead, I'm just a bullshit consumer destined to
acknowledge my ignorance in the world for the
adulterated
growth of corporate consumerism.

By the way,
this is bullshit too.

Ol' Bones

The
blues man's bones
bow
and
bob
to bend
and send
you
that feeling that
you,
oh so, want to know.

Savor
the sun's flame.

Dance insane.

Voodoo
hoodoo in
sweet candy sweat.

Feet barenaked
on a porch,
the brow
always
hangs
low
with a sly smile
under a tipped gentleman's hat
in the summer's heat with a beat.

You Say

Deliberate and long
were her eyelashes lashing
out.

She
saw me swaying
like a
beast against myself
in longing
for what will certainly not become.

Then she hid next to no one
as she started to stare into me,
her misery.

Me? I had thought.

Me? You knew me.

Me? You had said that
you had loved me, but
never do my words
attend
to what
you
say.

Skin

I am an empty pile of flesh.

Staring deeper into
the hole of my soul, I saw
the future,
the obvious fate.

Alive,
I was reborn
dead.

I am an empty pile of flesh.

Anything in between realities
exists as well as the realities
before
or
after.

Staring, still, deeper into
the hole of my soul, I saw
the past,
the oblivious fate.

Dead,
I was reborn
alive.

I am an empty pile of flesh.